I0774166

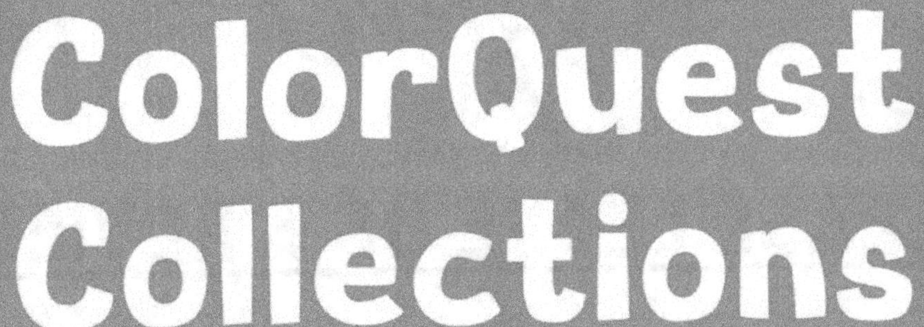

ColorQuest
Collections
Fun and creative coloring books
Calming | Relaxing | Stress Relief
For more fun and creative coloring books, search for ColorQuest Collections in your favorite bookstore!

Thank You

PLEASE LEAVE US A REVIEW!

IF YOU ENJOYED THIS COLORING BOOK, PLEASE TAKE A MOMENT TO LEAVE A REVIEW. YOUR FEEDBACK HELPS US IMPROVE AND GUIDES OTHER CREATIVE SPIRITS TO THEIR PERFECT COLORING ADVENTURE!

FOR MORE CREATIVE COLORING BOOKS, PLEASE SEARCH FOR COLORQUEST COLLECTIONS IN YOUR FAVORITE BOOKSTORE!

COLORQUEST COLLECTIONS

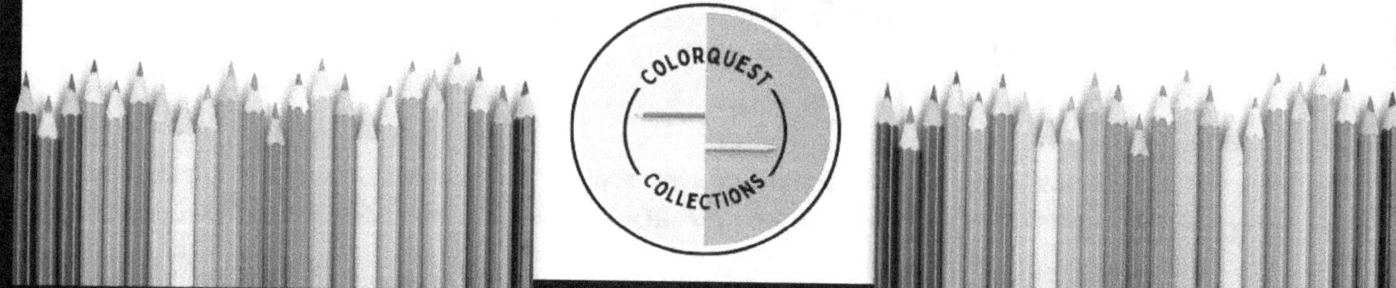